THE
PROHIBITION ERA

THE
PROHIBITION ERA

BY MARTIN GITLIN

Content Consultant

Jason S. Lantzer, PhD

Adjunct Professor of History, IUPUI and Butler University

ABDO
Publishing Company

CREDITS

Published by ABDO Publishing Company, 8000 West 78th Street, Edina, Minnesota 55439. Copyright © 2011 by Abdo Consulting Group, Inc. International copyrights reserved in all countries. No part of this book may be reproduced in any form without written permission from the publisher. The Essential Library™ is a trademark and logo of ABDO Publishing Company.

Printed in the United States of America,
North Mankato, Minnesota
062010
092010

Editor: Melissa Johnson
Copy Editor: Erika Wittekind
Interior Design and Production: Kazuko Collins
Cover Design: Kazuko Collins

Library of Congress Cataloging-in-Publication Data
Gitlin, Marty.
  The prohibition era / Martin Gitlin.
     p. cm. — (Essential events)
  Includes bibliographical references and index.
  ISBN 978-1-61613-685-7
  1. Prohibition—United States. 2. Drinking of alcoholic beverages—United States—History—20th century. I. Title.
  HV5089.G48 2010
  363.4'10973—dc22

                            2010013459

TABLE OF CONTENTS

Chapter 1	The Last Sip	6
Chapter 2	An Old Debate	16
Chapter 3	A Thirsty Public	28
Chapter 4	Hide and Seek	36
Chapter 5	Gangsters and Violence	44
Chapter 6	Police Corruption	54
Chapter 7	The Law Fights Back	62
Chapter 8	A Failed Experiment?	70
Chapter 9	The Time for Repeal	80
Chapter 10	Lessons of Prohibition	88
Timeline		96
Essential Facts		100
Additional Resources		102
Glossary		104
Source Notes		106
Index		109
About the Author		112

Billy Sunday preached against drinking alcohol.

THE LAST SIP

20-foot (6-m) coffin was on display. The funeral was about to begin. Preacher Billy Sunday prepared to give his eulogy. But there was something quite unusual about this ceremony. The "dead man," John Barleycorn, never existed. Yet 10,000 people were on hand not to mourn but, rather, to celebrate his death.

It was January 15, 1920. The following day, Prohibition would go into effect throughout the United States. The manufacture, sale, and transport of alcohol were about to become illegal through the Eighteenth Amendment to the Constitution. John Barleycorn was a fictional character from an English folk song. He stood for the evils of alcohol. And from a church in Norfolk, Virginia, Sunday was about to give Barleycorn a send-off. "Good-bye, John," Sunday told the huge gathering. "You were God's worst enemy; You were Hell's best friend. I hate you with a perfect hatred. . . ."[1]

Millions of people in the United States shared his hatred. To some of these people, alcohol production and consumption caused many of the nation's problems. But to many others, it was a simple moral issue. They believed the nation needed to rise above the use of intoxicating beverages. They argued that drunken behavior lowered the nation's standards and caused criminal activity. Some religious Americans believed that those who drank alcohol would not be accepted into heaven when they died. Sunday was among those who agreed. He continued:

A monument to the fictional John Barleycorn marked the beginning of Prohibition.

The reign of tears is over. The slums will soon only be a memory. We will turn our prisons into factories and our jails into storehouses and corncribs. Men will walk upright now, women will smile, and children will laugh. Hell will be forever for rent.[2]

Making Alcohol Illegal

Prohibition had been in effect in many areas of the United States for decades before it became a national law. By 1893, states in the Northeast including Maine, New Hampshire, and Vermont had outlawed alcohol, as had several conservative farming states such as South Dakota and Kansas. Parts of 13 other states were "dry," which was a common expression meaning alcohol was not allowed.

The movement to ban intoxicating beverages, which had started centuries earlier, continued to intensify. However, at least one powerful man was against an alcohol ban. That was U.S. President Woodrow Wilson, who favored an educational program that taught children the dangers of drinking alcohol and encouraged adults to consume in moderation.

Many Americans disagreed with Wilson. In August 1917, the U.S. Senate voted by an overwhelming 65–20 count to approve the Eighteenth Amendment, which banned alcohol in the United States.

Prohibition and World War I

The United States was involved in World War I from 1917 to 1918. During this time, the government enacted several laws that limited food consumption at home in order to better feed the soldiers at war. President Wilson used his wartime powers to prohibit distilleries from using grain to make hard liquor, and he lowered the alcohol content in beer to 2.75 percent alcohol.

On November 21, ten days after the war ended, Congress passed the Wartime Prohibition Act. It banned the manufacture and sale of all alcoholic beverages with more than 2.75 percent alcohol. This act remained in effect until the Eighteenth Amendment and the Volstead Act took its place.

On December 18, 1917, the House of Representatives followed as 70 percent of its members voted in favor as well.

Only one roadblock remained. For Prohibition to become part of the U.S. Constitution, three-fourths of the states' legislatures would have to approve the amendment within a seven-year period. Thirteen months after Congress passed it, on January 16, 1919, Nebraska became the thirty-sixth state to ratify the Eighteenth Amendment, making it part of the U.S. Constitution. At the time, the Eighteenth Amendment was the most quickly ratified amendment in U.S. history.

Refused to Ratify

After the needed 36 states ratified the Eighteenth Amendment, thereby turning it into a federal law, nine other states showed their support by doing the same. This meant that 45 out of the 48 states that existed at the time voted for Prohibition. Texas and Illinois never ratified the Prohibition bill, and Rhode Island specifically rejected it.

Lawmakers gave the country a year to put the new rules into effect. They set the date for January 16, 1920. At midnight on that date, the consumption, sale, and transportation of alcohol became illegal. January 17 would be the first full day of Prohibition.

Once the Eighteenth Amendment was added to the Constitution, Congress had to pass a law defining exactly what was illegal and what the

Many people across the country were in favor of outlawing alcohol.

penalties would be for breaking the law. That law was the National Prohibition Act, also called the Volstead Act. It set the legal limit for alcoholic beverages at 0.5 percent alcohol. Normally, beer averages about 5 percent alcohol, wine is about 10 to 12 percent alcohol, and hard liquor is about 40 percent alcohol or more. So, the law meant that only a tiny trace of alcohol would be allowed in any beverages.

President Wilson vetoed the Volstead Act, but Congress overrode his veto on October 28, 1919. Prohibition had become the law of the land.

Still-Legal Drinking

There were exceptions to the law, most of which were included as political compromises to get the law passed. For example, the Volstead Act allowed for wine to be used for religious purposes in churches and synagogues. At the time, it was commonly believed that alcohol used in moderation led to good health. Accordingly, alcohol remained legal for some medicinal purposes.

The Volstead Act also included a "personal use" clause. This meant that those who still had alcohol in their homes could drink it under their roofs, but once it ran out, they could not purchase any more. The day before Prohibition started, a federal judge ruled that any alcohol stored outside a private home could be taken away. People who believed they could store it in warehouses and safe deposit vaults outside their homes suddenly discovered they were mistaken. The result was a

Short and Sweet

The Eighteenth Amendment was just three paragraphs long, approximately 100 words total. It stated simply that making, selling, and transporting alcohol was illegal. It said that three-quarters of the states needed to ratify it for it to become law.

The Volstead Act, on the other hand, contained 66 sections and was so confusing that some believed it was the reason the Eighteenth Amendment failed. The Volstead Act included several political compromises that watered down the original intent of the reformers but allowed it to pass Congress. Some of these compromises, such as allowing prohibition enforcement officers to be hired without passing a government exam, also contributed to the failure of Prohibition.

mad rush as people fetched what they had stored in public places and brought it back to their homes. Meanwhile, eager Prohibition agents searched cities with bats and sledgehammers, ready to smash bottles and kegs of alcohol wherever they could be found. In addition, some states put in place stricter laws that prohibited some of these exceptions.

Although millions celebrated the birth of the Prohibition Era, millions of others grieved. Most of the latter were those who simply enjoyed drinking. The majority of them drank responsibly and in moderation. Whether at home or in bars, they believed that consuming alcohol made social

Volstead and Wheeler

The National Prohibition Act of 1919 was also known as the Volstead Act because Minnesota Representative Andrew J. Volstead introduced it.

The driving force behind the National Prohibition Act was Wayne Wheeler, a leader of the Anti-Saloon League. Wheeler's hatred of alcohol stemmed from a childhood incident in which a drunken worker on his father's Ohio farm plunged a pitchfork into his leg. Wheeler became a fierce advocate of banning alcohol. He lobbied politicians to join the crusade. His efforts helped make large parts of Ohio dry by 1908. He even charged that the U.S. brewery industry was aiding the enemy during World War I. He pointed out that the industry was greatly controlled by Germans who were not yet U.S. citizens.

Wheeler eventually wrote the National Prohibition Act and handed it to Volstead to introduce it. Though Volstead was not as strongly antialcohol, Wheeler was confident the politician would be able to get the act passed.

situations better. People who manufactured alcohol, such as beer brewers, liquor distillers, and winery owners, lost their jobs. Many bars and saloons went out of business.

On January 16, hours before Prohibition took effect, former U.S. Secretary of State William Jennings Bryan spoke in front of hundreds of members of Congress and thousands of other onlookers during a celebration in Washington DC. Bryan celebrated the end of the liquor industry, which he blamed for ruining the lives of children:

> They are dead, that sought the child's life. . . . They are dead! They are dead! King Alcohol has slain more children than [Biblical tyrant] Herod ever did. . . . As we grow better and stronger through the good influence of Prohibition, we will be in position to give greater aid to the world.[3]

German Beer Drinking

The popularity of beer in the United States can be traced back to German immigration, which began in earnest in 1832. Beer drinking was common among German Americans, and breweries sprung up in cities where they lived, mostly in the Midwest. These included Chicago, Illinois, Milwaukee, Wisconsin, St. Louis, Missouri, and Cincinnati, Ohio. Milwaukee is often considered the beer capital of the United States.

During World War I, as the United States fought Germany, many Americans turned against all things German. The association between beer and Germans was one factor in turning public sentiment against alcohol and beer during this time.

A group of men take their last legal sip of beer before Prohibition goes into effect.

An early nineteenth-century image depicts demons producing alcohol.

An Old Debate

The campaign against alcohol in the United States began more than two centuries before the beverage was outlawed nationally in 1920. The first prohibition law in the American colonies took effect in Georgia in 1735. It was ended eight years later because farmers were ignoring their crops to focus on moonshining and bootlegging, the production and sale of homemade liquor.

But even before that, some people in the American colonies called for moderation in what became known as the temperance movement. In early eighteenth-century Massachusetts, public shame was used to convince people to stop undesirable behaviors. A person who was considered a drunkard and a hazard to society might be forced to wear a large *D* on his or her clothing so the entire community would know.

Increase Mather and his son Cotton, members of the Puritan religion, began preaching against the use of alcohol for religious reasons as early as 1673. The Methodists, another religious group, took up the fight as well. Drinking was so widespread in society that they called for moderation, not prohibition.

Many religious people, however, opposed any level of alcohol use. They claimed drunkenness made one less fearful of God. A court in Philadelphia, Pennsylvania, noted in 1744 that heavier amounts of drinking in society were linked with swearing and poverty and encouraged people to give up religion.

Such views were certainly in the minority during that period. People drank alcohol instead of water in areas where water quality was poor. Because much of the country had poor roads, it was much easier to transport alcoholic products made from fruits and grains than to transport the crops themselves.

Alcohol was an important part of social and political life as well. Politicians were used to buying alcohol for potential voters. In 1758, for example, George Washington spent a large sum of money on alcohol that he passed out to voters when he sought election in Virginia's House of Burgesses. His actions were common among politicians until well into the nineteenth century.

RUSH AND BENEZET

Dr. Benjamin Rush, a Revolutionary War hero, and Anthony Benezet, a member of the Quaker religion, gave the temperance movement a scientific base. Benezet, who also had a medical background,

Jefferson and Alcohol

Thomas Jefferson, the third president of the United States, started disliking hard alcohol after he left office. He felt the country would be run more effectively if some politicians drank less:

"The habit of using [hard alcohol] by men in public office has often produced more injury to the public service, and more trouble to me, than any other circumstance. . . . And were I to [become president] again, with the knowledge I have acquired, the first question that I would ask with regard to every candidate for office should be, 'Is he addicted to [liquor]?'"[1]

Dr. Benjamin Rush believed that drinking alcohol led to crime and disease.

argued against the widely held claim that alcohol had medicinal value. He argued that it made the sick sicker and that it was addictive, it led to memory loss, and it caused both physical and moral breakdown.

Benjamin Rush

Dr. Benjamin Rush was not only involved in the temperance movement. He was ahead of his time in the humane treatment of mental illness as well. Rush also detested slavery in an era in which that view was still unpopular. He formed the nation's first antislavery society. He also spent a large portion of his own money to open a school for African-American children.

Rush produced a pamphlet in 1784 linking heavy drinking with criminal activity, disease, and punishments such as prison and even hanging. But even Rush did not support prohibition. Rather, he urged that drinkers should switch from hard liquor to beer and wine. At that time, fermented drinks such as beer and wine were not considered "alcoholic" in the same way as hard liquor.

Changing Views

Early in the nineteenth century, distilleries were established in many parts of the country. Farmers producing grains such as barley, rye, and corn used their crops to make whiskey, which in the 1820s cost between 25¢ and 40¢ per gallon (3.8 L). After 1800, people began drinking more outside the home and becoming intoxicated more often. Some historians link this behavior change to the Industrial Revolution, which drastically changed the work and daily lives of many Americans. This rise in alcohol consumption, accompanied by a rise in crime, violence, and poverty, encouraged the early temperance movements.

One major factor in the growth of early temperance movements was a religious revival known as the Second Great Awakening, which occurred between 1795 and 1837. The religious groups that grew out of this movement emphasized each person's responsibility to reform the world. Encouraging temperance was one way members of these religious groups wanted to make society better. These new groups also encouraged the active involvement of women, something that many earlier groups had not allowed. Taking on more important roles in religious life gave women speaking and leadership skills that transferred to the temperance movement.

Alcohol Use Increases

How much did alcohol use increase in the United States from 1792 to 1810? In 1792, 2,579 registered distilleries in the country produced approximately 5.2 million gallons (19.7 million L) of liquor. During that year, annual consumption averaged approximately 2.5 gallons (9.5 L) for every man, woman, and child in the United States.

Eighteen years later, the number of distilleries had grown to 14,191. The average consumption of alcohol per American had risen to 4.5 gallons (17 L) a year.

Scientists determined in the 1820s that alcohol was in fact present in fermented drinks such as beer and wine. By the 1830s, some temperance groups including the American Temperance Society were calling for people to give up all alcohol, not just hard liquor. Total avoidance of alcohol became known as teetotalism.

Meanwhile, the U.S. population and its demand for alcohol were growing. A wave of immigrants from Germany in the 1840s, in particular, brought with it a love of beer and a desire to establish a brewing industry in the United States. As immigrants poured in from Europe, they came together in saloons, which were businesses that allowed people to gather and drink alcohol. Thousands of saloons sprang up throughout the country.

The saloons were more than drinking establishments. They were also places where men in the community could come together to socialize and discuss news and politics. Many saloons even provided a free lunch, though the food was heavily salted to encourage heavier drinking. Saloon owners were important in their communities, and many used alcohol and community connections to become politicians.

Teetotalers

Those who drank no alcohol both before and after Prohibition were known as *teetotalers*. The word, which originated around the time of the American Civil War, can be traced to a group called the American Temperance Society. The society insisted that its members abstain from drinking and marked their names on its membership list with a *T* that stood for "total." Soon people began putting the *T* and *total* together and came up with the word *teetotaler* to describe those who refused to drink.

German immigrants brought with them a strong drinking and saloon culture.

However, because some saloons encouraged gambling and prostitution, many people came to view saloons as places that encouraged vice. Meanwhile, the saloons and the liquor industry fought any attempts by politicians to put regulations on them.

Yet despite it all, drinking actually decreased during the mid-1800s. Alcohol had become a moral issue. Religious leaders called not for moderation, but for the total prohibition of alcohol. Another group, called the Washingtonian Temperance Society, attracted working-class people to the temperance movement, many of whom were previously hard drinkers. Washingtonianism was successful because it provided aid to families as well as social interaction to replace the saloon culture. However, many people who joined soon started drinking again.

Prohibition Sentiment Spreads

A shift was occurring—temperance was no longer seen as a purely moral problem that called for reformers to encourage self-control. Instead, reformers began pushing for laws that would punish those who did not uphold these moral standards. In 1851, Maine outlawed the manufacture and sale of liquor. Prohibition laws were quickly adopted in many states, including New York, Oregon, Minnesota, Michigan, Rhode Island, Pennsylvania, and Massachusetts. But that did not signal the end of drinking in those states. Liquor was still easily imported from other states and consumed at home. Home brewing also gained popularity.

The debate over alcohol became less important during the American Civil War (1861–1865), but it became a hot topic again in the war's aftermath. Leading the newest fight against alcohol were women, many of whom had husbands who were alcoholics or had wasted money or lost jobs due to alcohol.

One powerful organization was the Women's Christian Temperance Union, which was founded in 1874. A strong-willed Kansan named Carry Nation was one influential member who emerged from the group in the late 1880s.

Kansas had become the first state to make Prohibition part of its constitution in 1881, but the law was largely ignored. In 1900, Nation began bursting into saloons throughout the state, smashing up bars, windows, and kegs of rum and whiskey with a large hatchet. A large woman who stood six feet

The Nation Sensation

Carry Nation was born Carry Moore in 1846. Her mother was committed to a mental hospital because she believed she was Queen Victoria of England. Nation herself believed in ghosts and communication with the dead. She claimed to have talked to Jesus Christ. She also experienced convulsions and depression.

She married a doctor named Charles Gloyd, who she discovered on her wedding day was an alcoholic. She gave birth to a daughter with disabilities and blamed her daughter's condition on her husband's smoking and alcohol use. They separated, and he died soon after. After marrying David Nation, a preacher and lawyer, she claimed Jesus commanded her to take action against saloons. She gained fame by smashing them up with hatchets.

Public interest in her eventually faded. She tried to earn a living reenacting her saloon raids on stage. She traveled to England for a speaking tour, but few people showed up. After a mental breakdown, she died in a mental hospital at age 65.

(1.8m) tall, Nation was so wild and frightening
that nobody dared to try to stop her. Soon she
was destroying saloons in St. Louis, Missouri,
Cincinnati, Ohio, Philadelphia, Pennsylvania, and
New York City. She became one of the most famous
people in the Prohibition debate.

Nation was not alone in the fight. In 1893, an
organization formed that would wage a less violent
but still effective battle to shut down saloons across
the country. That organization was the Anti-
Saloon League. The league consisted of a national
partnership of a variety of groups that wanted to
shut down saloons. The league was not linked to
any particular religion. There were groups for
men, for women, for different racial and ethnic
groups, and for rural and urban people. The
national organization coordinated the efforts of the
various groups to make changes at the local level.
The individual groups worked to close saloons or
tighten liquor laws in their city or county. As the
laws became more widespread, the groups pushed for
statewide action. As the new century began, the Anti-
Saloon League and other temperance groups began
to push for nationwide prohibition of alcohol.

Carry Nation led a crusade against saloons.

A temperance reformer recording the people who entered a saloon. Women were crucial members of the temperance movement.

A Thirsty Public

The movement to ban alcohol was growing more popular by the turn of the twentieth century. The Anti-Saloon League had become a lobbying powerhouse, convincing politicians of the need to fight for the prohibition of alcohol.

The organization only backed candidates who shared its views.

Meanwhile, many of the same women who were working for a constitutional amendment to give women the right to vote also strongly backed the abolition of alcohol. It is no coincidence that the Eighteenth Amendment starting Prohibition and the Nineteenth Amendment giving women the right to vote were ratified just months apart.

In addition, millions of other Americans believed drunkenness was at least partly responsible for many of the country's problems. Political cartoons in favor of temperance reform often attached social problems including disease, poverty, and crime to alcohol use. A majority of Americans had embraced that view of alcohol by the early twentieth century.

Even though Prohibition gained more support in the southern and western states and far less in the large Midwestern cities, it was no surprise when the Eighteenth Amendment passed Congress and was ratified just over one year later. But it was also no surprise that people still desired intoxicating beverages. As Prohibition went into effect, the illegal manufacturing and sale of alcohol began throughout the country.

Law Breaking Begins

First Liquor Theft

How long after the Volstead Act took effect did it take for the first theft of liquor to be recorded? Less than one hour. On January 17, 1920, six armed, masked bandits sneaked into a Chicago railroad-switching yard, tied up the night watchman, and emptied two freight cars full of whiskey that was intended for medicinal purposes. The alcohol was worth $100,000.

Prohibition was enforced to different degrees in different areas of the country. Some cities, counties, and states were quite strict, but others tended to look the other way when alcohol laws were broken. In general, Prohibition was more generally accepted in rural areas and more likely to be ignored in urban areas. The nation's first Prohibition commissioner, John F. Kramer, promised to enforce the law:

In cities large and small, and in villages, and where it is not obeyed it will be enforced. . . . We shall see to it that [liquor] is not manufactured. Nor sold, nor given away, nor hauled in anything on the surface of the earth or under the earth or in the air.[1]

Despite the words of warning, many people ignored the new law. During the first five months of Prohibition, more than 500 court cases involving violations of the Volstead Act took place in Chicago alone. That city's physicians had issued 300,000 illegal prescriptions for alcohol.

Quickly, a new type of drinking establishment came into existence. They were called speakeasies because they operated in secret, so patrons were supposed to "speak easy" about them in public. Speakeasies cropped up throughout the country, many in large cities.

Many cities and counties had once had laws that prohibited saloons from operating too closely to churches, schools, or residential areas. With Prohibition in place, the illegal speakeasies did not respect the old boundaries, and they moved into areas where they were previously not allowed.

The most notorious town for illegal drinking was Chicago. It has been estimated that more than 7,000 speakeasies opened in that city from 1920 to 1922. Gangsters most often ran the establishments that attracted the highest-class patrons.

Women of Business

Two of the most successful speakeasy owners in New York City during Prohibition were women. Both ran high-class businesses. One was Belle Livingstone, who had been married and divorced four times and was friends with European royalty. She wore red Chinese lounging pajamas in her establishment and often rejected customers who had poor manners.

The other was Mary Louise "Texas" Guinan, who had moved to New York from Waco, Texas. She had been married three times and had spent part of her career as a circus bronco rider and as an actress in western movies. She told jokes and put on musical acts, encouraging the audience to participate. According to legend, the Prince of Wales once hid in the kitchen at her club and pretended to be a chef during a police raid.

Most speakeasies hid behind legitimate businesses. They operated in basements or in the backs of restaurants, drugstores, or hardware stores. The more glamorous ones were in makeshift nightclubs. One New York speakeasy even hid behind a fake Jewish synagogue. In that city, there were 15,000 legal drinking establishments prior to Prohibition but 32,000 illegal ones after the Eighteenth Amendment took effect.

Why were so many illegal bars and clubs able to operate?

The Story of George Remus

Perhaps the most clever lawbreaker during the Prohibition era was lawyer and German-born immigrant George Remus. Remus received a license to sell medicine in his twenties, well before Prohibition, and later became an attorney. He was making approximately $45,000 a year in that field, which was a large amount at the time. Prohibition would give him the opportunity to increase that number many times over.

Following the enactment of the Eighteenth Amendment, Remus sold his law practice. He moved from Chicago to Cincinnati and sunk his life savings of $100,000 into purchasing whiskey certificates, drug stores, and the largest distilleries in the United States. He obtained a government license and claimed to be selling alcohol to drug companies that were licensed to sell it for medicinal purposes, which would have been legal.

However, Remus had secretly purchased those drug companies, so he was actually selling the alcohol to himself. And though he did bottle some of the alcohol for medicine, most of it ended up in speakeasies and in the hands of private clients and others who sold or drank it illegally. Remus was eventually caught, but not before he made approximately $40 million.

One reason was that they were well hidden and too numerous to track down. But a more disturbing reason was corruption. The police were often bribed to leave speakeasies alone. Illegal payoffs also protected individuals and businesses that earned money through the manufacture, sale, and transportation of alcohol.

Police inspectors in the United States generally received a salary of a couple thousand dollars a year during the 1920s. But in one year during Prohibition, one inspector in Philadelphia took in $193,000 and another earned $102,000 in illegal payoffs. A police captain made $133,000. An estimated 1,600 Prohibition enforcement agents were fired for crimes such as bribery, extortion, theft, forgery, and perjury.

Home Brewing

People making alcohol at home presented an even more difficult enforcement challenge than the speakeasies. Some drugstores sold blocks of dried grape concentrate called wine bricks. The packaging contained a label warning users it was illegal to mix yeast and water with the brick because that would create wine. It was an open secret that nearly everyone who purchased these items was doing so to make wine at home.

Meanwhile, hardware stores began selling homemade stills in which alcohol could be produced. Some people transformed their bathtubs into stills. The Prohibition Bureau, a government agency, estimated that in 1929 alone, Americans produced approximately 700 million gallons (2.6 billion L) of liquor in such makeshift stills.

Home brewing, however, could be dangerous or even fatal. Some people desperate to drink would use anything with alcohol in it to create homemade liquor—including embalming fluid, rubbing alcohol, and even antifreeze. Both outside and inside homes, whiskey was produced in unsanitary conditions. Poisonous alcohol resulted in thousands of deaths across the country during Prohibition. ⁓

Moonshine Monikers

Illegal liquor manufacturers came up with some creative names for their products. Among them were Panther Whiskey, Red Eye, Cherry Dynamite, Old Stingo, Old Horsey, Scat Whiskey, Happy Sally, Jump Steady, Soda Pop Moon, Sugar Moon, Jackass Brandy, White Mule, and Squirrel Whiskey. The last one was given that name because it was so strong it supposedly made its drinkers climb trees.

Men drinking together in a speakeasy during Prohibition

Smugglers unloading illegal alcohol on a pier in New York City

HIDE AND SEEK

With U.S. breweries and distilleries closed, the demand for alcohol was high enough that people could make a lot of money importing alcohol into the country illegally. The people who smuggled alcohol into the United States were known as rumrunners. Smuggling was a quick but dangerous way to make money. Their exploits avoiding the law took on a heroic, romantic air for some people.

Alcohol was legal in almost every other country. It was shipped in from countries such as France, Great Britain, and Germany, but Mexico and Canada were the most convenient sources. Liquor could be purchased cheaply in the French islands of St. Pierre and Miquolon off the Canadian coast. Gin was 25¢ a quart (0.9 L), rum 50¢ a gallon (3.8 L), and champagne a dollar a bottle. Those islands experienced great economic benefits from the rum-running trade during Prohibition.

Many fishermen realized they could make far more money hauling illegal alcohol than legal fish. Hundreds of boats would line up in international waters a few miles off the Atlantic Coast to receive the shipments. In fact, the scene was so commonplace that the line of boats off New York Harbor became known as Rum Row.

Rumrunners gained a reputation for courage and a devil-may-care lifestyle. They were always in danger. As soon as they crossed into U.S. waters three miles (4.8 km) off the mainland, they were fair

game for searches or attacks by the
U.S. Coast Guard and Prohibition
agents. But even more frightening
were pirates, who would wait for a
purchase to be made and then board
a ship by gunpoint, steal the money,
and sometimes even kill the crew.

THE REAL McCOY

The most legendary rumrunner
was Bill McCoy, who coined a well-
known expression by describing the
high-quality alcohol he brought
into the United States as "the real
McCoy."[1] He earned $15,000 on his
first run in 1921 and soon was able to
afford a boat he named the *Arethusa*.
He made millions of dollars bringing
liquor in from the Bahamas, where
whiskey cost a mere eight dollars a
case.

McCoy did not drink, but he
offered what he claimed to be the
best liquor around. He took great
precautions to hide the illegal

More Profit Than Fishing

How did the residents
of New Bedford, Massa-
chusetts, know that local
fishermen had begun
dealing in the illegal
liquor trade? They could
tell the fishermen were
making a lot more money
than they did by catching
and selling fish. One New
Bedford resident claimed:

"You knew right away
when a man stopped fish-
ing and started running
rum. . . . In the first place,
his family began to eat
proper and you could tell
by what they bought at
the grocery store."[2]

contents. He packaged the alcohol in pyramid-shaped, six-bottle burlap packs stitched closed with twine. By not using the large wooden cases used by other rumrunners, he saved a great deal of room, which allowed him to store more alcohol. The packaging also made the bottles less likely to break.

Accounts vary about how McCoy was finally caught, but according to some, McCoy was forced to give up the *Arethusa* to his crew and hide in a remote area sometime around 1923. He was back at the helm in November 1924, when the Coast Guard fired upon his boat off the coast of New Jersey. Rather than lose his beloved vessel, he surrendered and eventually went to jail.

Too Tough to Stop?

Coast Guard officers had their hands full. Their boats were often too slow to catch up with the speedboats operated by rumrunners. Those bringing illegal alcohol into the country often won the chase on the high seas. Although enforcement was better in some areas than others, the Coast Guard never managed to

No Fun Anymore

When Bill McCoy was released from jail following his conviction for rum-running, he was quoted as saying he would have returned to that illegal trade if the fun had not gone out of it. McCoy was referring to organized crime, which he felt had taken over the business. He was considered the most spirited and adventurous rumrunner of the 1920s.

intercept more than 5 percent of all rum-running traffic despite its approximately 11,000 agents.

The Coast Guard received little help from the government. When President Calvin Coolidge asked for resources to buy faster boats so the Coast Guard could keep up with the high-speed rumrunner craft, Congressmen who favored the repeal of Prohibition prevented it. In fact, it was later learned that some of those same politicians were being bribed by people involved in the rum-running trade.

Corrupt officers in the Coast Guard also

Motor Master McGhee

Many rumrunners could thank a man named Jimmy McGhee for their success in avoiding the Coast Guard. As Prohibition went on, the Coast Guard patrols gained experience and were given faster boats. McGhee helped keep smugglers one step ahead of the law.

McGhee was a motor mechanic who combined speedboats with engines taken from World War I fighter planes. His boats were capable of cruising along the water at 65 miles per hour (105 km/h). Coast Guard boats simply could not keep up. The McGhee boats ran on aviation fuel and required great skill to pilot. The powerful engines could easily overheat and blow up at top speed.

Though McGhee was an enemy to the Coast Guard, he could not be arrested because he never did anything illegal. He never bought, sold, or transported liquor.

McGhee, who taught himself the craft of engine mechanics, rejoined law-abiding society after the repeal of Prohibition. In fact, he became well known for his mechanical work in the auto-racing world and was hired as an adviser to a fighter aircraft company during World War II.

allowed smugglers to continue their illegal work. Rather than patrol the waters for illegal activity, these officers sometimes became smugglers themselves. Smuggling brought in far more money than their paychecks.

In late 1924, a Coast Guard officer named Captain Edward Gallagher was piloting picketboat *No. 203* when he met up with a rum-running vessel called the *Elias B.* about 35 miles (56 km) south of New York Harbor. Gallagher was not there to arrest the rumrunners. Instead, he helped them transport 700 cases of scotch and champagne into the harbor.

As policemen looked on, the cases were loaded into a truck owned by William Vincent Dwyer, who ran the rum-running business. The policemen were secretly on Dwyer's payroll.

Cop Turned Smuggler

One of the most successful West Coast smugglers was Roy Olmstead, a former police officer based in Seattle, Washington. Olmstead was kicked off the force early in the Prohibition era for dabbling in the illegal alcohol trade. He became a full-time rumrunner, purchasing whiskey and scotch from Canada and selling it for a huge profit. By 1922, it was estimated that he brought in 1.5 million gallons (5.7 million L) of whiskey from north of the border. Two years later, Olmstead was a millionaire.

U.S. Sales Overseas

Smuggling went both ways. U.S. distillers made money by selling whiskey overseas. They purchased whiskey certificates, which gave them permission to sell alcohol for medicinal purposes. Most of their overseas buyers were not taking whiskey for its medicinal qualities. One official who was aware of the trickery was Prohibition Commissioner Roy Haynes:

> *If we believed the tales of all who apply for liquor permits, we would naturally come to the conclusion that the whole world is sick. . . . Does anyone believe that Scotland, home of whiskey, is really in need of 66,000 gallons (250,000 L) of American whiskey?*[3]

Few believed these flimsy cover stories. When there was money to be made ignoring the Volstead Act, however, little got in the way of illegal activities.

Government inspectors making records of alcohol seized from smugglers

*This large still was confiscated by federal agents. Bootlegging was
a lucrative activity for gangsters.*

GANGSTERS AND VIOLENCE

ang warfare in the United States can be
traced back more than a century before
the Prohibition era. But when the clock struck 12:01
a.m. on January 17, 1920, marking the beginning
of Prohibition, gang warfare intensified. The desire

for alcohol meant there were billions of dollars to be made illegally. Gangsters, particularly in the country's biggest cities, battled each other with sometimes deadly results. By late in that decade, dangerous criminals such as Al "Scarface" Capone, Dutch Schultz, and Gus "Bugs" Moran had become household names.

Illegal Activities

In the 1920s and early 1930s, criminals and gang members participated in various illegal ventures. The most lucrative activity was bootlegging. Bootlegging was the process of manufacturing, transporting, and selling liquor. The money to be made from bootlegging was enormous. Speakeasies, private dealers, and ordinary citizens all wanted alcohol and were willing to pay high prices for it. Bootlegging was not as common in the first years of Prohibition because the networks for smuggling and selling were not yet in place. Soon, however, the business increased.

The gang bosses were not secretive about their actions. They received plenty of support from politicians, policemen, and even judges to continue bootlegging. Violence became far more common as Prohibition wore on and the law frequently turned a blind eye.

Hijacking liquor was a common activity among gangsters. The criminals would steal stocks of alcohol at gunpoint, which resulted in a huge profit for the thieves and a financial disaster for the victims. Liquor hijackings often led to further violence, as the victims sought revenge on the thieves.

AL CAPONE

Of all the gangsters who operated during Prohibition, none is better remembered than Chicago's Al Capone. Alphonse Capone was born and raised in New York. His parents had arrived in the United States from Naples, Italy, in 1893, six years before his birth.

Capone grew up in a tough neighborhood where he first experienced gang warfare. He was a member of two gangs—the Brooklyn Rippers and Forty Thieves Juniors. Although he was a bright boy, he did not apply himself to his schoolwork, and he dropped out of school in sixth grade. He committed petty crimes with his gangs as a teenager, although he did find legitimate work as a pinsetter in a bowling alley.

As he became a more hardened criminal, Capone joined the notorious Five Points Gang in the New York borough of Manhattan. He worked in gangster Frankie Yale's bar as a bouncer and a bartender. It was there that Capone earned his nickname "Scarface" after he was cut up during a brawl.

Capone committed his first murders in New York. He killed

The Story of "Big Jim"

The father of twentieth century gangs in Chicago was a flamboyant native Italian nicknamed "Big Jim" Colosimo. He began his career as a petty pickpocket and eventually became a millionaire by running a string of brothels. He was also involved in gambling, extortion, and other criminal activities.

When Colosimo was threatened in 1909, he summoned nephew Johnny Torrio from New York for protection. The three men who had endangered Colosimo were soon found dead.

When Prohibition became the law of the land, Colosimo remained content to stay out of bootlegging. Torrio, however, yearned to make big money from it. The relationship soon deteriorated. Just four months after the start of Prohibition, Torrio asked his uncle to accept two truckloads of whiskey into his restaurant, Colosimo's Cafe. Colosimo entered the cafe and was shot to death by an unknown gunman.

Later investigations never established the murderer, but a witness description indicated that it was a New York friend of Torrio's named Frankie Yale. It is believed that Torrio hired Yale to kill Colosimo. Despite his reputation as a criminal, Colosimo was given a hero's funeral. The thousands of mourners that attended his funeral included judges, prominent businessmen, and politicians.

Al Capone was one of the most notorious gangsters during Prohibition.

two gang rivals and badly injured another in 1919.
Soon after, he moved to Chicago to avoid police and
revenge seekers. He quickly attracted the attention
of Chicago mob boss Johnny Torrio, who believed
Capone had potential as a gang leader. Torrio was
among Chicago's first bootlegging and speakeasy
kingpins. Torrio soon made Capone his top
accomplice, as well as a full partner in his saloon and
gambling businesses.

Soon after Capone arrived, Torrio was shot and
injured by rivals, causing him to leave Chicago.

Capone catapulted to the top of the gang. Capone was trusted and well liked by his men. He showed a better ability to organize than Torrio had and proved particularly effective in keeping the law on his side through bribes and intimidation.

Public Enemy Number One

By the mid-1920s, Capone controlled speakeasies, gambling houses, horse racing tracks, distilleries, breweries, and even brothels. His reported annual income was approximately $100 million.

Capone was more in danger from vengeful rivals than he was from politicians or policemen. His many spies, including cops, maintained a careful watch for potential enemies. And when a threat was found, Capone had the enemy murdered.

Despite all the gangland killings, Capone was never tried in court for any violent crime. He always had an alibi. He was arrested in 1926 for the murders of three people, but he was released from jail after one night due to a lack of evidence. Yet, in 1930 he was placed atop a list of Chicago's 28 most dangerous criminals and selected as "Public Enemy Number One."

Gang Rule

The violence increased throughout the 1920s. Approximately 800 gang members were murdered in New York City alone during Prohibition. The man who organized much of the illegal activity was Arnold Rothstein, who first made his mark setting up a rum-running operation with boats smuggling alcohol in from Canada and the islands off the Florida coast.

Before long, Rothstein had attracted gangsters with such colorful names as Waxey Gordon, Big Maxie Greenberg, and Lucky Luciano to form the most powerful gang in New York City. Rothstein's group did most of its work nonviolently by negotiating deals. Other gangs were much more likely to use violence. The notorious Dutch Schultz ruled the Bronx in New York City. Police estimates claimed the Schultz gang was responsible for 138 murders.

Despite the violence surrounding gang warfare, many of the gang leaders operated out in the open.

McSwiggin Killing

One man who got too close to the world of Chicago gangsters and paid for it with his life was young attorney William McSwiggin. McSwiggin, the son of a police sergeant, was in the wrong place at the wrong time in 1926. He was the victim of a drive-by shooting as he stood outside a bar called the Pony Inn. He was friends with two of Al Capone's criminal rivals—Jim Doherty and Tom Duffy—who were shot and killed at the same time. Most gangland murders were no longer big news in Chicago by that time, but the McSwiggin killing made the front page of the newspaper.

Capone was foremost among them. He claimed that by breaking the law of Prohibition he was just providing the public with what it wanted. And he did his best to endear himself to the people of Chicago. He even opened up a soup kitchen for the destitute in 1929 as the Great Depression was beginning to destroy the lives of many Americans. But in reality, Capone was a ruthless killer.

St. Valentine's Day

One of Capone's most notorious and violent crimes became known as the St. Valentine's Day Massacre. Capone's men murdered several members of Bugs Moran's gang in the most famous slaughter in Prohibition-era history.

Moran, who owned a string of speakeasies, was challenging Capone for gang supremacy in Chicago. One day he decided the Old Log Cabin whiskey he was receiving from Detroit-based bootleggers under Capone's control was too expensive. He informed Capone he would begin looking for his whiskey elsewhere.

Moran's customers hated the new whiskey he was selling, so Moran asked Capone to supply him again with Old Log Cabin. Capone, however, had found higher-paying customers. And since whiskey was in short supply, he refused Moran's request.

Moran's gang then hijacked Capone's stock of Old Log Cabin. Capone was angry. And people who angered Capone usually wound up dead. Capone sent a phony message to Moran, claiming a batch of Old Log Cabin whiskey had been sent to a garage on North Clark Street. Soon several of Capone's men, including two dressed in police uniforms, were on their way there.

Moran's men were waiting for their boss in the bitter cold on February 14, 1929, St. Valentine's Day. Moran was not there. A black car pulled up in front of the garage, and four Capone gang members hiding sawed-off shotguns and machine guns emerged. They walked into the garage and gunned down seven of Moran's gang in cold blood.

Increasing gang activity had been accepted by many as an outgrowth of Prohibition. Even so, the St. Valentine's Day Massacre sickened the nation. —

Bugs Moran

Bugs Moran was raised in Chicago and became involved in gangs during his teenage years. He committed at least 20 burglaries and landed in jail three times before the age of 21. Moran was a member of Deanie O'Banion's gang, which controlled the North Side. He took over the operation in 1927 and, despite his murderous activities, gained a reputation for his sense of humor.

Following the repeal of Prohibition, he lost much of his power. By the mid-1930s, he had moved to Ohio, where he started robbing banks. He died of lung cancer in jail in 1957.

Graphic images from the St. Valentine's Day Massacre shocked the nation.

Al Capone, right, at a football game with a former Chicago alderman in 1931—an example of friendly relations between gangsters and government.

POLICE CORRUPTION

*I*n some U.S. cities, it seemed almost as though Prohibition had been repealed because city leaders were doing little or nothing to stop alcohol sales or gang activity. New York Congressman Fiorello LaGuardia, who later became the mayor of New York City, had warned that Prohibition would be impossible to administer: "In order to enforce Prohibition . . . it will require a police force of 250,000 men and a force of 250,000 men to police the police."[1]

He was right. By 1922, approximately 5,000 speakeasies had opened for business, and gangsters were competing to provide alcohol for them and for anyone else who would pay for it.

Citizens found they could purchase it whenever they pleased. There were thousands of sellers disguised as legitimate merchants. Wrote Michael A. Lerner in *Dry Manhattan: Prohibition in New York City*:

> *Organized crime's control of the liquor trade was so efficient that New Yorkers came to treat alcohol as just another commodity despite its illegality. Though New Yorkers knew of the corruption and violence [related] to the alcohol trade, they had come to accept purchasing liquor on a daily basis as a routine practice, hardly [different] from buying flowers or groceries.*[2]

Taking Bribes

Chicago Mayor Bill Thompson and his police force were not merely ignoring the alcohol trade and

Maryland Congressman J. P. Hill openly defied prohibition laws by serving alcohol in his home.

the violent gangster activity surrounding it. They were also encouraging it by taking bribes.

Many Prohibition Bureau agents, who were supposed to enforce the law, gave in to temptation. They knew taking bribes from gangsters or getting involved in the alcohol trade themselves paid more money than their regular paychecks.

A mere ten days after the Volstead Act became the law of the land, three agents were arrested in Chicago for accepting bribes and selling confiscated liquor. Two months later, two agents in Baltimore were arrested for similar offenses. Nearly every month for the next ten years, one or more employees of the Prohibition Bureau were arrested for crimes such as assault, bribery, theft, drunkenness, and lying under oath. In the 1920s, 1,587 bureau workers were fired for various offenses.

Mayor Thompson officially left behind savings and property worth $150,000 upon his death in 1944. However, safe deposit boxes in his name carried cash, stocks, and gold certificates worth a total of almost $2 million. Most suspected a large portion of that money was earned from bribes and other illegal activities during Prohibition.

One example of how Chicago politicians even promoted ruthless killers revolved around gangster Deanie O'Banion. Before Al Capone came forward as the most powerful gangster in Chicago, O'Banion was the leading criminal in the city. His flower shop was a front for his bootlegging business. By the time he was murdered, he had been credited with 25 gangland killings.

Not Such a Hero

One of many supposedly reputable Chicagoans who got mixed up with gangsters was *Chicago Tribune* reporter Alfred J. Lingle. When Lingle was shot down, the newspaper's coverage described him as a hero. It claimed he was murdered while investigating gangsters. But it was soon revealed that Lingle lived a lavish lifestyle despite a weekly salary of only $65 and worked as an intermediary between gangsters and the police. When he was killed, Lingle was even wearing a diamond-studded belt Capone had given him.

O'Banion, however, was close enough to politicians that in 1924 the Democratic Party held a dinner for him. Attending the party were not only some of the most prominent gang members of Chicago but also Chief of Detectives Michael Hughes and several other of the city's top law enforcement officials. O'Banion was so powerful that the Democrats presented him with a platinum watch set in rubies and diamonds in the hope that he would help their candidates win the upcoming election.

The result of police neglect was a shocking deterioration of

Poison, Alcohol, and Death

During Prohibition, Americans discovered the dangers of taking the production of alcohol away from legitimate manufacturers. The liquor made by moonshiners and bootleggers was often unsafe. Illegal producers sometimes mixed in industrial ingredients used in paint or household cleaning products. The result was often illness or even death.

Bootleg liquor was so concentrated with alcohol that it was estimated to be ten times more potent than the average pre-Prohibition liquor. But it was the deadly poisons that made it lethal. According to author and Prohibition expert Thomas Coffey, the death rate from poisoned liquor reached epidemic proportions. By 1925, the death rate had soared to 4,154, approximately four times the total from five years earlier.

One person angered by that statistic was humorist Will Rogers, who believed the U.S. government was allowing it to happen. "Governments used to murder by the bullet only," he said. "Now it's by the quart."[3]

Though deaths related to poisonous alcohol soared in cities such as Philadelphia and Chicago, they were even more common in less populated areas, where real liquor was harder to obtain.

law and order. Chicago was a noted gangster hotbed before the enactment of Prohibition. Crooks were always involved in illegal gambling and other activities, but not until the Eighteenth Amendment was ratified did blood really begin to flow in the streets. From 1920 to 1933, nearly 800 gangsters were murdered in battles between rivals.

The courts did little to stop gang violence. Of the 136 gangland murders that occurred in Chicago in the first five years of Prohibition, only six resulted in trials and all but one of those ended in the accused being set free. The only guilty gangster who was convicted had killed a rival inside a police station.

The Genna Family

If not for the cooperation of the police force, 50 percent of which Capone once claimed was on his payroll, Chicago gangsters would never have been able to operate so freely. This truth revealed itself through six bootlegging brothers of the Genna family: Angelo, Antonio, Michael, Peter, Sam, and Vincenzo.

The Gennas started by purchasing industrial alcohol with a government license. The liquid was contaminated with poisons such as wood alcohol. It was hardly filtered or redistilled before it was flavored and sold as whiskey. The liquor could be lethal, but the Gennas sold it anyway.

An Effective Law?

Some trends in the early Prohibition years indicated the new law was working. In its first two years, hospitals reported fewer cases of alcohol-related illnesses, and law enforcement officials claimed there was a drop in crimes involving alcohol. Meanwhile, the ward of Chicago's Cook County Hospital that treated alcoholism closed, and fewer arrests led to one wing of the Chicago City Jail shutting down. Soon, however, the illegal bootlegging industry began to flourish, and drinking picked up again.

The process of making and bottling the alcohol was done in relative secrecy in private homes. The Genna warehouse, on the other hand, sat just four blocks from the Maxwell Street police station. The Gennas made no attempt to hide what they were doing. The odor coming from the warehouse was unmistakable, and large delivery trucks were coming and going 24 hours a day.

When the law raided the place, the Gennas were given 24 hours notice. The Gennas even paid officers from the Maxwell Street precinct to protect their liquor trucks from rival gangsters. Nearly 200 uniformed cops were transferred elsewhere after an investigation revealed the payoffs.

Vincent Genna, a member of the feared Chicago crime family, in 1929

This drugstore was shut down for one year after its owner was caught violating prohibition laws.

THE LAW FIGHTS BACK

aw enforcement officials who ignored or even participated in gangster activity made it impossible for Prohibition to work. But many officers worked to enforce the Eighteenth Amendment and risked their lives in the process.

Among them was a portly New Yorker named Isidor Einstein, who was earning a meager $40 a week as a postal clerk when the country went dry in 1920. The 40-year-old had a wife, four kids, and an elderly father to support, so he took a slightly better paying job as a Prohibition agent.

Einstein was fluent in four languages and could speak a little Russian and Chinese. A believable actor who could speak with any foreign accent, he would dress up in different costumes so as not to be recognized and then visit various illegal drinking establishments and order liquor. When it was served to him, he would give the bartender his standard line: "There's sad news here. You're under arrest."[1]

Einstein carried a gun but never used it. Einstein, who worked with partner Moe Smith, played various undercover roles. He pretended to be a homeless person begging to come in from the cold to enter one speakeasy. He dressed up in a football uniform and played an athlete celebrating a victory to get served a drink in a club frequented by the sporting crowd. He introduced himself as an actor to prompt the bartender to offer him some liquor at a private theatrical club. He even showed up with a line of fresh-caught fish at a bar where the patrons

Izzy Einstein, top right and bottom left, *and Moe Smith,* top left and bottom right, *in plain clothes and in costume.*

were mostly fishermen. One scam featured Einstein pretending to be a friend of Smith, who played an out-of-towner. They would order a meal at a New

York restaurant, and then Einstein would ask Smith in a rather loud voice what play he wanted to see. Smith would reply loudly enough for the waiter to hear that what he really wanted was a drink. The waiter would soon produce some alcohol, only to be arrested.

THE UNTOUCHABLES

Einstein made 4,932 arrests as a Prohibition agent. But a different agent, Eliot Ness, made the most important arrest of all. His men were called The Untouchables. The gangster they brought down was Al Capone.

Ness was born in Chicago in 1903. He was a teenager when his city became the gangster capital of the United States. After earning a degree in criminology, he joined the U.S. Treasury Department and was assigned to the Chicago office of the Bureau of Prohibition. He was soon placed in charge of cutting off alcohol supplies and shutting down breweries owned by Capone.

Wiretaps

How did Eliot Ness and The Untouchables gain information about where Al Capone and other crooks were doing business? They hired and trained wiretapping experts who could listen in on phone conversations during which gangsters planned their bootlegging and other illegal activities. The wiretapping brought tremendous success.

To aid in this dangerous assignment, Ness sought only men who could not be corrupted. Capone attempted to bribe Ness's men, but his offers were refused. Soon Chicago newspapers were calling Ness and his helpers "untouchables." The name became legend.

Ness and The Untouchables began a series of raids on stills and alcohol distribution centers. Through the media, Ness attempted to reverse the image of Capone as a modern-day Robin Hood who cared about the people of Chicago and instead sought to expose the gangster as a murderer and criminal.

Ness might have preferred to nab Capone for murder or bootlegging. In the end, although Capone was eventually charged with 5,000 violations of the Volstead Act, he was actually arrested for tax evasion. Capone began an 11-year sentence in 1932.

DEFENDING PROHIBITION

Such successes in the enforcement of the Volstead Act were rare enough that Prohibition Commissioner Roy Haynes felt motivated to defend the law in a 1926 book called *Prohibition Inside Out.* In it, he claimed bootleggers were increasingly on the run, but he also admitted it was difficult for Prohibition agents to resist temptations such as bribes. He added that one group of brewers offered agents a huge sum of $300,000 a week to look the other way.

Haynes pointed out that only 43 of some 4,000 Prohibition agents had been convicted in the courts from 1920 to 1925, proving that 99 percent of the force was honest. However, others pointed out that during the 1920s, 1,587 agents were fired for questionable actions in the line of duty.

Ness after Prohibition

Eliot Ness gained fame leading The Untouchables in Chicago, but the rest of his career was relatively quiet. After Prohibition was repealed in 1933, he was sent to the mountains of Ohio, Kentucky, and Tennessee as an alcohol tax agent, but a year later he was transferred to Cleveland, Ohio. It was there that he accepted a job overseeing the city's police and fire departments. He clamped down on organized crime and police corruption in Cleveland.

Ness threw all his energy into his work, but that badly affected his personal relationships. He was married three times and divorced twice.

In the end, Ness and The Untouchables were best known for standing up to Al Capone, which few others had the courage to do. His fame grew through self-publicity and the media. He wrote an autobiography titled *The Untouchables* in 1957, which was immediately turned into a television series of the same name. He died that same year. In 1987, a movie titled *The Untouchables* became a nationwide hit.

Even Haynes, however, seemed discouraged by the illegal activities involving so-called respectable citizens in many areas of the country. Most of the gangster killings were occurring in New York and Chicago, but the Eighteenth Amendment was being ignored in many places around the nation.

The mayor of Atlanta was sentenced to 18 months in jail for participating in a bootlegging ring. In one Midwestern city, the mayor, sheriff, city court judge, and police were all involved in the illegal alcohol trade. In California, a bank president and a representative of the Internal Revenue Service went to jail in a case involving liquor worth $4 million.

By the mid-1920s, Americans were drinking 200 million gallons (757 million L) of hard liquor, 684 million gallons (2.6 billion L) of malt liquor (strong beer), and 1.2 billion gallons (4.5 billion L) of wine per year. Bootleggers were taking in an annual profit of $4 billion.

Prohibition was not working. And by the early 1930s, some of the same people who had fought for Prohibition 15 years earlier were speaking out against it. The call for repeal was gaining momentum. ⌐

*Eliot Ness and his incorruptible agents worked to shut down
Al Capone's operation in Chicago.*

*People crowded this New York speakeasy during Prohibition.
The police lacked the resources to stop people from drinking.*

A Failed Experiment?

The United States was not prepared
to enforce Prohibition. The national
government, the states, and the local authorities
all lacked the resources to enforce liquor laws. Jails
and prisons filled up, and the courts fell behind

in hearing cases. In places where the law was not popular, juries rarely ruled against the defendant—in many cases because the jury members were breaking the liquor laws themselves. Several states, including New York, even passed laws by 1925 that prohibited local police from investigating alcohol violations.

The glamour associated with clubs and speakeasies made drinking more appealing to many. Others drank in defiance of the law because they felt the government had no right to regulate their decision to drink alcohol. In general, people drank more hard liquor and less beer because beer had less alcohol per volume and therefore it was more difficult to transport and hide.

POISON IN THE ALCOHOL

By the late 1920s, it had become apparent that Prohibition was not eliminating alcohol consumption and indeed might have been increasing it. In addition, people were dying in great numbers from contaminated alcohol. In 1926, 750 people died from alcohol poisoning in New York City alone. In 1927, an estimated 50,000 Americans died the same way.

The problem was that liquor was being made from denatured alcohol, or pure alcohol to which methanol, a poison, has been added. Denatured alcohol is used to make certain industrial products. Denatured alcohol could be obtained legally during Prohibition. Some bootleggers redistilled the alcohol to remove the poison, but others failed to do so.

In 1927, the *New York Telegram* decided to investigate. Reporters collected more than 500 samples of liquor purchased from 400 speakeasies. Fifty-five of them contained significant amounts of methanol, and other less dangerous poisons were discovered in 70 more.

Shifting Opinion

Right before the Eighteenth Amendment was passed, the majority of Americans backed the law. But after several years of seeing it in action, many people's views changed dramatically. From 1927 forward, according to some opinion polls, more than three-fourths of Americans favored repeal.

The methanol in alcohol killed thousands of Americans during Prohibition. Yet the Anti-Saloon League lobbied against putting poison labels on denatured alcohol. The head of the league's public relations, Wayne Wheeler, was criticized severely for playing a role in those deaths. But he seemed to believe that those who drank illegally during Prohibition got what they deserved. He said:

The government is under no obligation to furnish people with alcohol that is drinkable when the Constitution prohibits it. The person who drinks this industrial alcohol is a deliberate suicide.[1]

FADING SUPPORT

By the late 1920s, several anti-Prohibition groups were making their voices heard. The Moderation League was made of middle-class citizens who had no connection to the liquor industry. The legal community, led by the American Bar Association, and worker organizations, such as the American Federation of Labor, also called for an end to Prohibition.

Yet the time to repeal had not come. In the 1928 presidential election, Republican and noted dry politician Herbert Hoover easily defeated Democrat Al Smith, who campaigned to return alcohol laws to local control. Those who backed Prohibition were encouraged by the

Beer for the Workingman

Although American Federation of Labor President Samuel Gompers stopped short of calling for bringing back hard liquor, he did tell the U.S. Senate:

"Depriving the American workingman of his glass of beer tends to promote industrial unrest and discontent."[2]

Gompers warned that in Detroit, Michigan, a radical organization called the Industrial Workers of the World was winning over factory employees. He believed the organization was dangerous and claimed Prohibition was partly to blame.

Herbert Hoover, center, was against drinking alcohol.

results. However, Hoover's win was more the result of his positions on other issues, not solely his views on Prohibition.

The road to repeal seemed long. Though support for ending Prohibition was gaining steam, 13 states would have to vote for repeal for it to be overturned. Isidor Einstein claimed that "Prohibition is here to stay" and that it would remain the law of the land

for "our lifetime at least."[3] Clarence
Darrow, the nation's foremost
attorney, stated humorously that 13
states voting to end the Eighteenth
Amendment was as likely as a man
"taking his summer vacation on
Mars."[4]

THE GREAT DEPRESSION

As it turned out, Prohibition
would not last much longer. Easily
the most significant factor in the
overturn of the law was economic.
The 1920s had been good financially
for most Americans. The U.S.
economy thrived. At first, some
attributed the economic prosperity
to Prohibition. They believed
production had increased and worker
problems had decreased because of
antialcohol laws. But signs of national
financial instability began to show
late in the decade. On October 29,
1929, the stock market crashed.
As banks toppled, many people

The Wickersham Commission

Among Herbert Hoover's
first acts as president in
1929 was to establish a
panel to assess the Vol-
stead Act. Led by noted
lawyer George Wicker-
sham, it became known
as the Wickersham
Commission. The group
submitted its final report
in 1931. Though only one
of the 11 commissioners
supported repeal, seven
others called for changes
in the Volstead Act. One
of these was the possibil-
ity of letting each state
decide whether it wanted
to continue trying to
enforce the law.

lost their life savings. Lives were ruined. And the crisis deepened until the country was in the worst economic depression in its history.

The Great Depression strengthened the movement to repeal Prohibition. As Americans lost jobs, homes, and money, they further questioned the wisdom of Prohibition. The nation needed the money normally collected from liquor taxes. Some of the many out-of-work Americans could have filled the thousands of jobs the alcohol industry had once provided—from brewers and winemakers to bartenders and truckers. The more the economy fell apart, the less sense the law seemed to make. Even those who had been the strongest advocates of a dry nation were changing their minds.

Meanwhile, dry leaders who had spearheaded the effort since the nineteenth century were growing old and dying, and no one was taking their place. With the goal of a constitutional amendment accomplished, the movement lost its forward momentum. Rather than educating people about the dangers of alcohol, the dry leaders instead spent the 1920s focused on enforcing the alcohol ban. Members of the new generation did not share the concerns of the old.

ORGANIZING AGAINST PROHIBITION

The Association Against the Prohibition Amendment (AAPA) fought to repeal Prohibition. The AAPA was as powerful a force against the Eighteenth Amendment as the Anti-Saloon League had been for it during the previous decade.

The AAPA worked to elect politicians who would vote for the repeal of Prohibition. Its members included some of the wealthiest and most influential corporate

---

Women Lead the Charge

Prohibition likely would not have become law without the strong backing of women. But by the late 1920s, many women were leading the fight for repeal. The most visible was Women's National Republican Club founder and president Pauline Sabin.

Sabin grew disenchanted with the Republican Party during the 1928 convention. Led by soon-to-be President Herbert Hoover, the Republicans were strongly against repeal. So she announced her resignation as the only woman in the Republican National Committee in order to work on modifying liquor laws. She then organized the Women's Organization for National Prohibition Reform (WONPR), which quickly gained 300,000 members and boasted more than 1 million by 1932.

Sabin and other leaders of the WONPR disobeyed the law by drinking wine or even martinis at parties. That led pro-Prohibition writer Ida Minerva Tarbell to express her disdain.

"Tea parties have become cocktail parties," she complained. "These insidious and sinister ladies at the bar are too sinister a fact to deny. . . . They are spreading a fatal poison."[5]

If Tarbell meant they were encouraging anti-Prohibition sentiment, she was correct. The WONPR continued to work until the law was repealed.

executives in the country. And when John D. Rockefeller—one of the richest men in the world—called for repeal in 1932, the end was in sight. The oil baron had been firmly against alcohol consumption for years. He explained:

> I was born a teetotaler, and I have been a teetotaler all my life. Neither my father nor his father ever tasted a drop of intoxicating liquor. [But Prohibition has brought] an evil even greater than [drinking], namely a nationwide disregard for law.[6]

The writing was on the wall. The law that some believed would last forever was about to be repealed less than 14 years after it was enacted.

Mass demonstrations against Prohibition took place in the early 1930s.

*With many people out of work or homeless during the Great Depression,
Prohibition became a less-important issue politically.*

THE TIME FOR REPEAL

resident Herbert Hoover and challenger
Franklin D. Roosevelt had many spirited
debates as they campaigned for the presidency in
1932. But hardly a word was said about Prohibition.
The main reason was that the Great Depression had

grown into the overwhelming issue. People who had lost all of their savings or who did not know where their next meal was coming from were not worried about the legality of drinking liquor. Another reason for the lack of discussion about Prohibition was that both Hoover and Roosevelt agreed the law was not working.

They may have agreed, but they differed on the details. Roosevelt favored complete repeal across the nation. Hoover, a dry advocate in 1928, believed in 1932 that each state should decide for itself whether to allow drinking. But neither candidate could ignore opinion polls showing that Americans overwhelmingly called for the end of Prohibition. Prohibition was briefly mentioned on the campaign trail when Roosevelt declared he was in favor of repeal in his acceptance speech for the Democratic nomination for president. He further showed his support by telling a crowd in St. Louis that the government could make millions of dollars by taxing beer.

Farmers for Repeal

One segment of U.S. society that reversed its position on Prohibition was the farming community. This usually conservative group was in the forefront of the fight to end legalized drinking, but changed its tune as the Great Depression began to take a toll on agriculture. Farmers pushed for repeal, which would again allow them to grow and sell the grains and hops brewers used to make alcohol.

Most Americans believed Hoover was not doing enough to relieve their economic suffering, and the result was a landslide victory for Roosevelt. The time for repeal was quickly approaching.

Moving toward Repeal

Wisconsin Senator John J. Blaine took the first step. On December 6, 1932, he proposed the states vote on adopting the Twenty-first Amendment, which would cancel the Eighteenth Amendment. After Congress passed the amendment on February 20, 1933, two-thirds of the states would have to ratify it. Roosevelt did not wait to get the alcohol industry moving again. He signed a bill on March 22, 1933, to modify the Volstead Act to legalize 3.2 percent beer, which had less alcohol in it than regular beer. The law went into effect on April 7.

The dwindling number of pro-Prohibitionists made one last stand. New York Women's Christian Temperance Union Vice President Mamie Colvin held up a loaf of bread, a bottle of milk, and some children's toys and proclaimed children would be without those items if Prohibition were repealed. She argued that people would spend their money on liquor rather than food or gifts for their families.

Roosevelt signed a bill on March 22, 1933, to relax prohibition laws.

Her words and those of her fellow dry leaders no longer carried much weight. On the first day of legal drinking since 1920, Americans drank an estimated 1.5 million barrels of beer. There were shortages of beer the next day, as breweries just starting up production could not keep up with demand.

A feeling of joy swept over some parts of the nation as bands played and people marched. At the Anheuser-Busch Brewery in St. Louis, 30,000 beer lovers surrounded company trucks that paraded down 20 blocks of the city.

Going from Dry to Wet

Many who once favored Prohibition changed their earlier views as crime went on. Among them was Ira L. Reeves, a Prohibition administrator from New Jersey. In his 1931 book *Ol' Rum River: Revelations of a Prohibition Administrator*, Reeves listed a number of "ifs" that were keys to making Prohibition work. His list was a way of explaining why it was not working:

If we can get honest men to enforce it.
If such men will remain honest. . . .
If people will not patronize the bootleggers.
If people will assist the authorities by tattling against their neighbors.
If it can be made a moral issue and not a political one.
If thousands of church members will stop being hypocrites . . . voting dry and drinking wet.
If all these ifs can be realized, or if a few of them can be vitalized, there might be some measure of hope; but I do not know how that end is to be accomplished, and I do not believe anyone else can offer a solution.[1]

The speed with which the states ratified the Twenty-first Amendment was stunning. By early December 1933, only a year after it was sent to the states for votes, 35 had ratified it.

The End of the Eighteenth Amendment

When one more ratification was needed, Americans looked to Utah. In fact, Utah's convention waited to vote because its members wanted to be the ones who officially ended Prohibition. At exactly 5:32 p.m. on December 5, Utah voted for repeal. Less than two hours later, Roosevelt signed the Twenty-first Amendment into law.

Americans were rather quiet on the first night following repeal. After all, the end of Prohibition had become a foregone conclusion by that time. And they had already celebrated when 3.2 percent beer was again legalized. In addition, few were in the mood for merrymaking when the country continued to be gripped by the Great Depression, which seemed to worsen daily. Many speakeasies closed for the night. Their owners, who had been breaking the law for a decade or more, did not want to get into trouble for operating without a business license. People who expected that the end of Prohibition would have a dramatic effect were mistaken— the night the law was repealed, few instances of mass drunkenness were reported.

In the first few days after repeal, liquor and wine manufacturers that

Billy Sunday

Among those who gave up on fighting against repeal of Prohibition was preacher Billy Sunday. Sunday, whose elaborate "funeral" of John Barleycorn made news when the Eighteenth Amendment took effect, got tired of trying to convince folks not to drink. As repeal neared, he said he was going to concentrate on giving sermons about the Bible instead.

Dry Areas

The repeal of Prohibition at the end of 1933 did not mean the end of Prohibition everywhere in the United States. Some states did not vote for it and kept liquor illegal for decades. The last holdout was Mississippi, which finally reversed Prohibition in 1966.

were restarting production found it difficult to keep up with demand. So in New Jersey, Governor A. Harry Moore announced that speakeasies and other establishments that still had stocks of alcohol could sell them without a license. After all, he said, alcohol had been sold illegally in that state for 13 years. He did not think it made sense to make the drinking establishments wait several days for their licenses.

Liquor did not flow freely everywhere, however. Individual states and communities still had the right to regulate alcohol. Some areas remained totally dry. Other areas allowed alcohol consumption but regulated it by making laws about when and where it could be sold and drunk. Nearly eight decades after the repeal of Prohibition, counties in several states still remain dry and do not allow the sale of alcohol at any time. In addition, some states ban the sale of alcohol on Sundays. —

A crowd celebrated the repeal of Prohibition in 1933
by rolling out a barrel of beer.

WHICH DO YOU PREFER ?

BAD LIQUOR
BOOTLEGGING
BRIBERY
RACKETEERING
TAX EVASION
LAW-BREAKING

HONESTY
LEGAL DRINKING
FINE LIQUOR
TAX PAYING
NEIGHBORLINESS
PERSONAL LIBERTY

A post-Prohibition poster expressed some people's opinion about legal and illegal drinking.

LESSONS OF PROHIBITION

ollowing the passage of the Twenty-first Amendment, most Americans were ready to forget Prohibition and continue with their lives. The Great Depression and the need to find solutions to the worst economic crisis in U.S. history overwhelmed all other issues. But some people began asking questions and drawing conclusions about the failed law. And many of those same questions are still being debated today.

Human Behavior

People have always questioned whether it is possible to regulate human behavior. Most people agree that behaviors that harm others must be controlled. Few would argue against laws that punish crimes such as murder, assault, and theft. But should laws be created against activities or actions that generally hurt only the individual engaging in them?

There are laws to protect society from the harmful effects of drunken acts, including drinking and driving. But does the government have the right to regulate morality and pass a law against all drinking? At the end of the Prohibition era, many Americans felt the answer to this question was no.

Negative Effects

Although Prohibition may have made it more difficult for Americans to obtain alcohol legally, the law did not stop people from drinking. Instead of decreasing drunkenness, the law actually encouraged law breaking. The Mafia had existed before Prohibition, but the law led to hundreds of murders in some major cities and illegal moonshining, rum-running, and bootlegging throughout the country and beyond. The law also resulted in widespread political corruption and illegal acts among police officers and politicians. The government learned it can be impossible to enforce a law if there are not enough resources dedicated to it or if all levels of government do not work together.

Prohibition had some lingering negative effects on society. Prohibition fueled the rise of organized crime. Certainly, gangs existed before the enactment of the Eighteenth Amendment, but bootlegging and smuggling required planning and organization, which brought criminals together for a common purpose. It also increased competition between gangs. The result was increased violence and murder in most major cities.

Temperance after Repeal

The Women's Christian Temperance Union (WCTU), which was founded in 1873 and played a role in bringing about Prohibition, is still in existence. The WCTU continues to fight against alcohol abuse and is also concerned with controlling drugs, tobacco, and gambling. The organization defines *temperance* as "moderation in all things healthful; total abstinence in all things harmful."[1]

Prohibition also tested the morals of those hired to enforce it. When given the choice between getting rich illegally or staying poor legally, many chose to get rich. It is difficult to enforce a law if large numbers of people look the other way when it is broken. For a law regulating behavior to work, a majority has to agree with it. This was not the case during Prohibition.

CHANGES AND SUCCESSES

Prohibition and the temperance movements that preceded it had a lasting impact on U.S. society and culture. Prohibition organizations such as the Anti-Saloon League were among the first organized groups to practice what is now known as special-interest politics. Members of these organizations gathered together around their single cause and refused to vote for politicians who did not share their views on the single issue. They also organized many small, independent local groups into a national coalition. They sent

The Prohibition Party

The Prohibition Party has nominated a presidential candidate for every presidential election since it was founded in 1872. The Prohibition Party candidate received at least 150,000 votes in every election from 1884 through 1920. The totals have dwindled since then. Candidate Gene Amondson earned only a total of 653 votes in the 2008 presidential election.

lobbyists to Washington DC to influence lawmakers. Wayne Wheeler, a prominent member of the Anti-Saloon League, even wrote the Volstead Act. Later groups adopted the tactics of these organizations to further their own causes.

The years before and after Prohibition also brought changes to the lives of women. Women's work for Prohibition and other reform causes taught valuable political organizing skills, one of several factors that led to women gaining the right to vote. Prohibition also broke old social habits. The majority of saloons and drinking establishments were

---

MADD about Drunk Driving

One way in which drinking often injures others is when people who are drunk drive cars. Founded in 1980, the organization Mothers Against Drunk Driving (MADD) has taken a leading role in preventing drunk driving, particularly among teenagers. According to MADD, in 2009 a drunk driver killed someone every 45 minutes in the United States.

According to its own statistics, the group has greatly lessened the number of such tragedies. Since 1980, the number of annual fatalities due to drunk driving has decreased more than 50 percent. In 2008, an estimated 11,732 Americans were killed by alcohol-related crashes. That figure was down nearly 10 percent from the previous year.

MADD lists its objectives as stopping drunk driving, supporting the victims of drunk driving, and preventing underage drinking. According to the MADD Web site, 50 to 75 percent of those who have had their driver's license suspended for drunk driving continue to drive. And those who are caught drinking and driving for the first time have driven drunk an average of 87 times before.

once off-limits for women, but during Prohibition women were welcome in speakeasies.

According to some historians, Prohibition also broke down the old saloon system. During Prohibition, the higher prices of illegal alcohol discouraged working-class drinking. Many poorer laborers were simply unable to afford alcohol, even if they wanted it. The saloon lost its place as the primary social and political center for many men.

After the end of Prohibition, society continued to recognize the harm that alcohol can cause. In the twentieth century, alcoholism came to be seen as a disease rather than a moral failing. As such, doctors and support groups united to help alcoholics control addiction. Other groups, such as Mothers Against Drunk Driving (MADD), try to limit alcohol's negative impact on others. In the mid-twentieth century, the drinking age in many places was 18. By the 1980s, however, the drinking age across the country was raised to 21. In the twenty-first

Alcoholics Anonymous

Many alcoholics seeking help with recovery turn to Alcoholics Anonymous, which has been successfully helping people overcome alcohol addictions for about 75 years. Alcoholics Anonymous was a direct result of Prohibition. It was founded two years after the Eighteenth Amendment was repealed.

century, the debate on alcohol has focused on the legal drinking age and what can be done to decrease underage drinking. Eight decades after the repeal of Prohibition, Americans still consume alcohol—and still struggle with its effects. ⌐

*This Massachusetts community recently changed
its laws to allow liquor sales on Sundays.*

TIMELINE

1673	1735	1784
Puritan leader Increase Mather begins preaching against alcohol use.	The first prohibition law goes into effect in Georgia. It only lasts eight years.	Benjamin Rush publishes a pamphlet linking alcohol with crime and disease.

1874	1881	1893
The Women's Christian Temperance Union is founded.	Kansas becomes the first state to prohibit alcohol in its state constitution.	The Anti-Saloon League is established.

1830s

Temperance groups begin calling for people to stop drinking alcohol entirely.

1840s

European immigrants including Germans bring a saloon culture with them to the United States.

1851

Maine becomes the first state to pass a law outlawing the sale and manufacture of liquor.

1900

Women's Christian Temperance Union leader Carry Nation begins a series of raids on saloons throughout the country.

1917

Congress passes the Eighteenth Amendment to the U.S. Constitution on December 18.

1919

Three-fourths of the states ratify the Eighteenth Amendment by January 16.

TIMELINE

1919	1920	1928
The Volstead Act explaining prohibition laws is passed on October 28.	Prohibition officially takes effect at 12:01 a.m. on January 17.	Republican Herbert Hoover defeats Democrat Al Smith in the 1928 election, which was considered a defeat for anti-Prohibition forces.

1932	1932	1933
Franklin D. Roosevelt, who had called for repeal, defeats Herbert Hoover in the 1932 presidential election.	The Twenty-first Amendment to end Prohibition is introduced in Congress on December 6.	Congress passes the Twenty-first Amendment on February 20.

1929

Members of Al Capone's gang murder rivals from Bugs Moran's gang on February 14, in the St. Valentine's Day Massacre in Chicago.

1929

The stock market crashes on October 29. The Great Depression fully takes hold soon thereafter.

1931

The Wickersham Commission delivers its findings that Prohibition should not be repealed, but that it should be modified.

1933

President Roosevelt signs a modification of the Volstead Act on March 22, legalizing 3.2 percent beer.

1933

Utah becomes the thirty-sixth state to ratify the Twenty-first Amendment on December 5, ending Prohibition.

1980

Mothers Against Drunk Driving is founded.

ESSENTIAL FACTS

DATE OF EVENT

January 17, 1920, to December 5, 1933

PLACE OF EVENT

United States

KEY PLAYERS

❖ Temperance leader Carry Nation

❖ Anti-Saloon League leader Wayne Wheeler

❖ Minnesota Representative Andrew J. Volstead

❖ United States Senate and House of Representatives

❖ Gang leader Al Capone

❖ Prohibition Bureau and other law enforcement agencies

❖ President Herbert Hoover

❖ President Franklin D. Roosevelt

HIGHLIGHTS OF EVENT

❖ Many individual states passed prohibition laws in the second half of the nineteenth century.

❖ Prohibition took effect in 1920.

❖ Lack of resources and corrupt or overwhelmed law enforcement and court systems made Prohibition impossible to enforce.

❖ The well-publicized St. Valentine's Day Massacre in 1929 shined a spotlight on gangster activity in the major cities.

❖ Many Americans turned against Prohibition by the late 1920s and early 1930s.

❖ Prohibition was repealed on December 5, 1933.

QUOTE

"I was born a teetotaler, and I have been a teetotaler all my life. . . . Neither my father nor his father ever tasted a drop of intoxicating liquor. [But Prohibition has brought] an evil even greater than [drinking], namely a nationwide disregard for law." —*John D. Rockefeller*

ADDITIONAL RESOURCES

SELECT BIBLIOGRAPHY

Behr, Edward. *Prohibition: Thirteen Years that Changed America*. New York: Arcade Publishing, 1996.

Kobler, John. *Ardent Spirits: The Rise and Fall of Prohibition*. New York: G. P. Putnam's Sons, 1973.

Lerner, Michael A. *Dry Manhattan: Prohibition in New York City*. Cambridge, MA: Harvard University Press, 2007.

Pegram, Thomas R. *Battling Demon Rum: The Struggle for a Dry America, 1800–1933*. Chicago, IL: Ivan R. Dee, 1998.

FURTHER READING

Nishi, Dennis, ed. *Prohibition*. Farmington Hills, MI: Greenhaven Press, 2003.

Orr, Tamra. *People at the Center of: Prohibition*. San Diego, CA: Blackbirch Press, 2004.

Slavicek, Louise Chipley. *The Prohibition Era: Temperance in the United States*. New York: Chelsea House, 2009.

Web Links

To learn more about Prohibition, visit ABDO Publishing Company online at **www.abdopublishing.com**. Web sites about Prohibition are featured on our Book Links page. These links are routinely monitored and updated to provide the most current information available.

Places to Visit

Anti-Saloon League Museum
Westerville Public Library
126 South State Street, Westerville, OH 43081
614-882-7277
www.wpl.lib.oh.us/AntiSaloon
The story of the organization that helped enact Prohibition starting in 1893 is told here.

The Gangster Museum of America
113 Central Avenue, Hot Springs, AR 71901
501-318-1717
www.tgmoa.com
Learn about gangsters, particularly during the height of organized crime in the United States during Prohibition.

Untouchable Tours
Clark Street and Ohio Avenue, Chicago, IL, 60643
773-881-1195
www.gangstertour.com
Take a bus tour and experience Chicago the way it was during Prohibition. Learn more about gangsters such as Al Capone and Bugs Moran and visit where they once hung out.

Glossary

alcohol
An intoxicating liquid.

amendment
An addition to the U.S. Constitution that becomes law.

bootlegging
The act of manufacturing, transporting, or selling alcohol illegally.

brewery
A factory where beer is made.

Coast Guard
A U.S. military service that enforces laws at sea.

Congress
The lawmaking body of the U.S. government consisting of the Senate and the House of Representatives.

consumption
The act of eating or drinking.

depression
A period during which a nation experiences terrible economic conditions.

distilleries
Factories where hard liquor is made.

drunk
Feeling the effects of alcohol consumption.

gang
A group of people generally considered to be working together to perform illegal acts.

gangster
An individual taking part in illegal gang activities.

intoxicating
> Having the ability to make someone drunk.

liquor
> A distilled alcoholic beverage such as vodka or whiskey.

moonshining
> The act of producing illegal liquor.

notorious
> Famous, especially for something bad.

ratify
> To confirm by voting for approval.

repeal
> To undo.

rum-running
> The act of bringing illegal alcohol into a country through land, sea, or air.

saloon
> Another name for a bar, generally used in the late nineteenth and early twentieth centuries.

speakeasy
> A bar or club that sold alcohol illegally during Prohibition.

still
> An apparatus used to make alcohol.

teetotaler
> An individual who does not drink alcohol.

temperance
> The belief in abstaining from drinking alcohol.

Volstead Act
> The act of Congress in 1919 that implemented and explained the rules of Prohibition.

Source Notes

Chapter 1. The Last Sip
1. "Billy Sunday Speeds Barleycorn to Grave." *Nytimes.com.* 17 Jan. 1920. 28 Oct. 2009 <http://query.nytimes.com/gst/abstract.html? res=9B07E0DB1F38E533A25754C1A9679C946195D6CF>.
2. Edward Behr. *Prohibition: Thirteen Years that Changed America.* New York: Arcade, 1996. 82–83.
3. Ibid. 82.

Chapter 2. An Old Debate
1. John Kobler. *Ardent Spirits: The Rise and Fall of Prohibition.* New York: G. P. Putnam's Sons, 1973. 33.

Chapter 3. A Thirsty Public
1. John Kobler. *Ardent Spirits: The Rise and Fall of Prohibition.* New York: G. P. Putnam's Sons, 1973. 221.

Chapter 4. Hide and Seek
1. Edward Behr. *Prohibition: Thirteen Years that Changed America.* New York: Arcade, 1996. 136.
2. Ibid. 140.
3. Ibid. 133.

Chapter 5. Gangsters and Violence
1. John Kobler. *Ardent Spirits: The Rise and Fall of Prohibition.* New York: G. P. Putnam's Sons, 1973. 238.

Chapter 6. Police Corruption
1. Jay Maeder. "Hide and Seek." Excerpt from *Big Town Big Time.* New York: Sports Publishing, 1998. 46.
2. Michael A. Lerner. *Dry Manhattan: Prohibition in New York City.* Cambridge, MA: Harvard University Press, 2007. 262.
3. Mark Thornton. "Policy Analysis: Alcohol Prohibition Was a Failure." *Cato Institute.* 17 July 1991. 4 Oct. 2009 <http://www.cato. org/pub_display.php?pub_id=1017&full=1>.

Chapter 7. The Law Fights Back
1. John Kobler. *Ardent Spirits: The Rise and Fall of Prohibition.* New York: G. P. Putnam's Sons, 1973. 295.

Source Notes Continued

Chapter 8. A Failed Experiment?
1. Edward Behr. *Prohibition: Thirteen Years that Changed America.* New York: Arcade Publishing, 1996. 222.
2. United States. Cong. Senate. Subcommittee of the Committee on the Judiciary. *Hearings on Prohibiting Intoxicating Beverages.* 66th Cong., 1st sess. 3 vols. Washington, DC: Government Printing Office, 1919. 212. 3 Nov. 2009 <http://books.google.com/books?id=IgovA AAAMAAJ&printsec=frontcover&source=gbs_navlinks_s#v=onepage &q-&f-false>.
3. John Kobler. *Ardent Spirits: The Rise and Fall of Prohibition.* New York: G. P. Putnam's Sons, 1973. 341.
4. Ibid.
5. Ibid. 343.
6. Arthur Brisbane. "This Week." *Winthrop News.* 12 Oct. 1933. 8 Oct. 2009 <http://news.google.com/newspapers?nid=1023&d at=19331012&id=QUcMAAAAIBAJ&sjid=ZWMDAAAAIBAJ& pg=5865,1054104>.

Chapter 9. The Time for Repeal
1. Ira Reeves. *Ol' Rum River: Revelations of a Prohibition Administrator.* Chicago, IL: Thomas S. Rockwell Company, 1931. 365–366.

Chapter 10. Lessons of Prohibition
1. Women's Christian Temperance Union. "Welcome to the WCTU." 12 Oct. 2009 <http://www.wctu.org/index.html>.

INDEX

alcohol poisoning, 34, 58, 60,
71–73
Alcoholics Anonymous, 93
American Civil War, 22, 24
American Temperance Society,
21–22
Anti-Saloon League, 13, 26,
28–29, 72, 77, 91–92
Association Against the
Prohibition Amendment,
77–78

Barleycorn, John, 6–7, 85
Benezet, Anthony, 18–19
Blaine, John, 82
bootlegging, 17, 45, 47, 48, 51,
57, 58, 59, 60, 65, 66, 67,
68, 72, 84, 90
Bryan, William Jennings, 14

Capone, Al, 45, 46–52, 57, 59,
65–66, 67
Colosimo, "Big Jim," 47
Colvin, Mamie, 82–83
Coolidge, Calvin, 40
corruption, 33, 41, 45–46, 49,
54–60, 67, 68, 90, 91

Darrow, Clarence, 75
Dwyer, William Vincent, 41

Eighteenth Amendment, 7,
9–10, 12, 13, 29, 32, 59, 62,
68, 72, 75, 77, 82, 84, 85,
90, 93
Einstein, Isidor, 63–65, 74

Gallagher, Edward, 41
Genna family, 59–60
German drinking, 13, 14, 22
Great Depression, 51, 75–76,
80–81, 85, 88

Haynes, Roy, 42, 66–68
home brewing, 24, 33–34, 60.
See also moonshine
Hoover, Herbert, 73–74, 75,
77, 80–82

interest group politics, 91–92

Jefferson, Thomas, 18

Kramer, John, 30

LaGuardia, Fiorello, 54–55
Lingle, Alfred, 57

Index Continued

Mather, Cotton, 17
McCoy, Bill, 38–39
McGhee, Jimmy, 40
McSwiggin, William, 50
Methodists, 17
Moderation League, 73
moonshine, 17, 34, 46, 58, 90.
  See also home brewing
Moore, A. Harry, 86
Moran, Gus, 45, 51–52
Mothers Against Drunk
  Driving, 92, 93

Nation, Carry, 25–26
National Prohibition Act,
  10–11, 13. *See also* Volstead Act
Ness, Eliot, 65–66, 67
Nineteenth Amendment, 29

O'Banion, Deanie, 52, 57–58
Olmstead, Roy, 41

prohibition laws, 16–17, 24,
  25, 86
Prohibition Party, 91
Puritans, 17

Quakers, 18

Reeves, Ira, 84
religion, 17–18, 21, 23
Remus, George, 32
Rockefeller, John, 78
Rogers, Will, 58
Roosevelt, Franklin, 80–82, 85
Rothstein, Arnold, 50
rum-running, 36–41, 50, 90.
  See also smuggling
Rush, Benjamin, 18–20

Sabin, Pauline, 77
saloons, 14, 22–26, 31, 48,
  92–93
Schultz, Dutch, 45, 50
Second Great Awakening, 21
Smith, Al, 73
Smith, Moe, 63–65
smuggling, 36–42, 45, 50, 90.
  See also rum-running
speakeasies, 31–33, 45, 48, 49,
  51, 55, 63, 71–72, 85–86, 93
St. Valentine's Day Massacre,
  51–52
Sunday, Billy, 6–8, 85

Tarbell, Ida, 77
teetotalism, 22, 78
temperance movements, 17–26,
    90–91
Thompson, Bill, 55–57
Torrio, Johnny, 47, 48–49
Twenty-first Amendment, 82,
    84–85, 88

Untouchables, The, 65–66, 67
U.S. Coast Guard, 38–41

violence, 44–52, 55, 59, 68,
    90
Volstead Act, 9, 11–12, 13, 30,
    42, 56, 66, 75, 82, 92. *See
    also* National Prohibition Act
Volstead, Andrew, 13

Wartime Prohibition Act, 9
Washington, George, 18
Washingtonian Temperance
    Society, 23–24
Wheeler, Wayne, 13, 72–73, 92
Wickersham Commission, 75
Wilson, Woodrow, 9, 11
women, 21, 24–26, 29, 31, 77,
    82, 92–93
Women's Christian Temperance
    Union, 25, 82, 90
World War I, 9, 13, 14, 40

ABOUT THE AUTHOR

Martin Gitlin was a reporter for two newspapers in northeast Ohio for 20 years before becoming solely a freelance writer. During his two decades as a reporter, Gitlin won more than 40 awards, including first place for general excellence from the Associated Press in 1995. The Associated Press also named him one of the top four features writers in the state of Ohio in 2001. Gitlin has written approximately 20 books about sports and history.

PHOTO CREDITS

Library of Congress, cover, 3, 6, 8, 27, 74, 80, 97, 98; Getty Images, 11; Bettmann/Corbis, 15, 35, 36, 43, 44, 53, 56; North Wind Picture Archives, 16, 28, 96 (bottom); Ken Welsh/ Photolibrary, 19, 96 (top); Christie's Images/Corbis, 23; AP Images, 48, 54, 79, 83, 99 (top), 99 (bottom); Chicago History Museum/Getty Images, 61, 87; Underwood & Underwood/Corbis, 62; Time & Life Pictures/Getty Images, 64; Hulton Archive/Getty Images, 69; Margaret Bourke-White/Time & Life Pictures/Getty Images, 70; David J. & Janice L. Frent Collection/Corbis, 88; Lisa Poole/AP Images, 95